THE JPS B'NAI MITZVAH TORAH COMMENTARY

Va-'ethannan (Deuteronomy 3:23–7:11)
Haftarah (Isaiah 40:1–26)

Rabbi Jeffrey K. Salkin

The Jewish Publication Society · Philadelphia
University of Nebraska Press · Lincoln

INTRODUCTION

News flash: the most important thing about becoming bar or bat mitzvah isn't the party. Nor is it the presents. Nor even being able to celebrate with your family and friends—as wonderful as those things are. Nor is it even standing before the congregation and reading the prayers of the liturgy—as important as that is.

No, the most important thing about becoming bar or bat mitzvah is sharing Torah with the congregation. And why is that? Because of all Jewish skills, that is the most important one.

Here is what is true about rites of passage: you can tell what a culture values by the tasks it asks its young people to perform on their way to maturity. In American culture, you become responsible for driving, responsible for voting, and yes, responsible for drinking responsibly.

In some cultures, the rite of passage toward maturity includes some kind of trial, or a test of strength. Sometimes, it is a kind of "outward bound" camping adventure. Among the Maasai tribe in Africa, it is traditional for a young person to hunt and kill a lion. In some Hispanic cultures, fifteen year-old girls celebrate the *quinceañera*, which marks their entrance into maturity.

What is Judaism's way of marking maturity? It combines both of these rites of passage: *responsibility* and *test*. You show that you are on your way to becoming a *responsible* Jewish adult through a public *test* of strength and knowledge—reading or chanting Torah, and then teaching it to the congregation.

This is the most important Jewish ritual mitzvah (commandment), and that is how you demonstrate that you are, truly, bar or bat mitzvah—old enough to be responsible for the mitzvot.

What Is Torah?

So, what exactly is the Torah? You probably know this already, but let's review.

The Torah (teaching) consists of "the five books of Moses," sometimes also called the *chumash* (from the Hebrew word *chameish*, which means "five"), or, sometimes, the Greek word Pentateuch (which means "the five teachings").

Here are the five books of the Torah, with their common names and their Hebrew names.

- **Genesis (The beginning), which in Hebrew is Bere'shit (from the first words—"When God began to create").** Bere'shit spans the years from Creation to Joseph's death in Egypt. Many of the Bible's best stories are in Genesis: the creation story itself; Adam and Eve in the Garden of Eden; Cain and Abel; Noah and the Flood; and the tales of the Patriarchs and Matriarchs, Abraham, Isaac, Jacob, Sarah, Rebekah, Rachel, and Leah. It also includes one of the greatest pieces of world literature, the story of Joseph, which is actually the oldest complete novel in history, comprising more than one-quarter of all Genesis.
- **Exodus (Getting out), which in Hebrew is Shemot (These are the names).** Exodus begins with the story of the Israelite slavery in Egypt. It then moves to the rise of Moses as a leader, and the Israelites' liberation from slavery. After the Israelites leave Egypt, they experience the miracle of the parting of the Sea of Reeds (or "Red Sea"); the giving of the Ten Commandments at Mount Sinai; the idolatry of the Golden Calf; and the design and construction of the Tabernacle and of the ark for the original tablets of the law, which our ancestors carried with them in the desert. Exodus also includes various ethical and civil laws, such as "You shall not wrong a stranger or oppress him, for you were strangers in the land of Egypt" (22:20).
- **Leviticus (about the Levites), or, in Hebrew, Va-yikra' (And God called).** It goes into great detail about the kinds of sacrifices that the ancient Israelites brought as offerings; the laws of ritual purity; the animals that were permitted and forbidden for eating (the beginnings of the tradition of kashrut, the Jewish dietary laws); the diagnosis of various skin diseases; the ethical laws of holiness; the ritual calendar of the Jewish year; and various agricultural laws concerning the treatment of the Land of Israel. Leviticus is basically the manual of ancient Judaism.

> Numbers (because the book begins with the census of the Isra-
elites), or, in Hebrew, Be-midbar (In the wilderness). The book
describes the forty years of wandering in the wilderness and the
various rebellions against Moses. The constant theme: "Egypt
wasn't so bad. Maybe we should go back." The greatest rebellion
against Moses was the negative reports of the spies about the
Land of Israel, which discouraged the Israelites from wanting to
move forward into the land. For that reason, the "wilderness generation" must die off before a new generation can come into maturity and finish the journey.

> Deuteronomy (The repetition of the laws of the Torah), or, in
Hebrew, Devarim (The words). The final book of the Torah is,
essentially, Moses's farewell address to the Israelites as they pre-
pare to enter the Land of Israel. Here we find various laws that
had been previously taught, though sometimes with different
wording. Much of Deuteronomy contains laws that will be important to the Israelites as they enter the Land of Israel—laws
concerning the establishment of a monarchy and the ethics of
warfare. Perhaps the most famous passage from Deuteronomy
contains the *Shema,* the declaration of God's unity and uniqueness, and the *Ve-ahavta,* which follows it. Deuteronomy ends with
the death of Moses on Mount Nebo as he looks across the Jordan
Valley into the land that he will not enter.

Jews read the Torah in sequence—starting with Bere'shit right after Simchat Torah in the autumn, and then finishing Devarim on the
following Simchat Torah. Each Torah portion is called a parashah (di-
vision; sometimes called a *sidrah,* a place in the order of the Torah
reading). The stories go around in a full circle, reminding us that we
can always gain more insights and more wisdom from the Torah. This
means that if you don't "get" the meaning this year, don't worry—it
will come around again.

And What Else? The Haftarah

We read or chant the Torah from the Torah scroll—the most sacred
thing that a Jewish community has in its possession. The Torah is

written without vowels, and the ability to read it and chant it is part of the challenge and the test.

But there is more to the synagogue reading. Every Torah reading has an accompanying haftarah reading. Haftarah means "conclusion," because there was once a time when the service actually ended with that reading. Some scholars believe that the reading of the haftarah originated at a time when non-Jewish authorities outlawed the reading of the Torah, and the Jews read the haftarah sections instead. In fact, in some synagogues, young people who become bar or bat mitzvah read very little Torah and instead read the entire haftarah portion.

The haftarah portion comes from the Nevi'im, the prophetic books, which are the second part of the Jewish Bible. It is either read or chanted from a Hebrew Bible, or maybe from a booklet or a photocopy.

The ancient sages chose the haftarah passages because their themes reminded them of the words or stories in the Torah text. Sometimes, they chose *haftarah* with special themes in honor of a festival or an upcoming festival.

Not all books in the prophetic section of the Hebrew Bible consist of prophecy. Several are historical. For example:

The book of Joshua tells the story of the conquest and settlement of Israel.

The book of Judges speaks of the period of early tribal rulers who would rise to power, usually for the purpose of uniting the tribes in war against their enemies. Some of these leaders are famous: Deborah, the great prophetess and military leader, and Samson, the biblical strong man.

The books of Samuel start with Samuel, the last judge, and then move to the creation of the Israelite monarchy under Saul and David (approximately 1000 BCE).

The books of Kings tell of the death of King David, the rise of King Solomon, and how the Israelite kingdom split into the Northern Kingdom of Israel and the Southern Kingdom of Judah (approximately 900 BCE).

And then there are the books of the prophets, those spokesmen for God whose words fired the Jewish conscience. Their names are immortal: Isaiah, Jeremiah, Ezekiel, Amos, Hosea, among others.

Someone once said: "There is no evidence of a biblical prophet ever being invited back a second time for dinner." Why? Because the prophets were tough. They had no patience for injustice, apathy, or hypocrisy. No one escaped their criticisms. Here's what they taught:

> God commands the Jews to behave decently toward one another. In fact, God cares more about basic ethics and decency than about ritual behavior.

> God chose the Jews *not* for special privileges, but for special duties to humanity.

> As bad as the Jews sometimes were, there was always the possibility that they would improve their behavior.

> As bad as things might be now, it will not always be that way. Someday, there will be universal justice and peace. Human history is moving forward toward an ultimate conclusion that some call the Messianic Age: a time of universal peace and prosperity for the Jewish people and for all the people of the world.

Your Mission—To Teach Torah to the Congregation

On the day when you become bar or bat mitzvah, you will be reading, or chanting, Torah—in Hebrew. You will be reading, or chanting, the haftarah—in Hebrew. That is the major skill that publicly marks the becoming of bar or bat mitzvah. But, perhaps even more important than that, you need to be able to teach something about the Torah portion, and perhaps the haftarah as well.

And that is where this book comes in. It will be a very valuable resource for you, and your family, in the b'nai mitzvah process.

Here is what you will find in it:

> A brief **summary** of every Torah portion. This is a basic overview of the portion; and, while it might not refer to everything in the Torah portion, it will explain its most important aspects.

> A list of the **major ideas** in the Torah portion. The purpose: to make the Torah portion real, in ways that we can relate to. Every Torah portion contains unique ideas, and when you put all

of those ideas together, you actually come up with a list of Judaism's most important ideas.

› Two *divrei Torah* ("words of Torah," or "sermonettes") for each portion. These *divrei Torah* explain significant aspects of the Torah portion in accessible, reader-friendly language. Each *devar Torah* contains references to **traditional** Jewish sources (those that were written before the modern era), as well as **modern** sources and quotes. We have searched, far and wide, to find sources that are unusual, interesting, and not just the "same old stuff" that many people already know about the Torah portion. Why did we include these minisermons in the volume? Not because we want you to simply copy those sermons and pass them off as your own (that would be cheating), though you are free to quote from them. We included them so that you can see what is possible—how you can try to make meaning for yourself out of the words of Torah.

› **Connections:** This is perhaps the most valuable part. It's a list of questions that you can ask yourself, or that others might help you think about—any of which can lead to the creation of your *devar Torah*.

Note: you don't have to like everything that's in a particular Torah portion. Some aren't that loveable. Some are hard to understand; some are about religious practices that people today might find confusing, and even offensive; some contain ideas that we might find totally outmoded.

But this doesn't have to get in the way. After all, most kids spend a lot of time thinking about stories that contain ideas that modern people would find totally bizarre. Any good medieval fantasy story falls into that category.

And we also believe that, if you spend just a little bit of time with those texts, you can begin to understand what the author was trying to say.

This volume goes one step further. Sometimes, the haftarah comes off as a second thought, and no one really thinks about it. We have tried to solve that problem by including a **summary** of each haftarah, and then a mini-sermon on the haftarah. This will help you learn how these sacred words are relevant to today's world, and even to your own life.

All Bible quotations come from the NJPS translation, which is found in the many different editions of the JPS TANAKH; in the Conservative movement's *Etz Hayim: Torah and Commentary*; in the Reform movement's *Torah: A Modern Commentary*; and in other Bible commentaries and study guides.

How Do I Write a *Devar Torah?*

It really is easier than it looks.

There are many ways of thinking about the *devar Torah*. It is, of course, a short sermon on the meaning of the Torah (and, perhaps, the haftarah) portion. It might even be helpful to think of the *devar Torah* as a "book report" on the portion itself.

The most important thing you can know about this sacred task is: *Learn* the words. *Love* the words. Teach people what it could mean to *live* the words.

Here's a basic outline for a *devar Torah:*

"My Torah portion is (name of portion) _____,
   from the book of _____, chapter

_____.

"In my Torah portion, we learn that_____
   (Summary of portion)
"For me, the most important lesson of this Torah portion is (what
   is the best thing in the portion? Take the portion as a whole;
   your *devar Torah* does not have to be only, or specifically, on the
   verses that you are reading).
"As I learned my Torah portion, I found myself wondering:
   ➤ *Raise a question* that the Torah portion itself raises.
   ➤ *"Pick a fight"* with the portion. Argue with it.
   ➤ *Answer a question* that is listed in the "Connections" section of
     each Torah portion.
   ➤ *Suggest a question to your rabbi* that you would want the rabbi
     to answer in his or her own *devar Torah* or sermon.

"I have lived the values of the Torah by _____
(here, you can talk about how the Torah portion relates to your own life. If you have done a mitzvah project, you can talk about that here).

How To Keep It from Being Boring
(and You from Being Bored)

Some people just don't like giving traditional speeches. From our perspective, that's really okay. Perhaps you can teach Torah in a different way—one that makes sense to you.

> Write an "open letter" to one of the characters in your Torah portion. "Dear Abraham: I hope that your trip to Canaan was not too hard . . ." "Dear Moses: Were you afraid when you got the Ten Commandments on Mount Sinai? I sure would have been . . ."
> Write a news story about what happens. Imagine yourself to be a television or news reporter. "Residents of neighboring cities were horrified yesterday as the wicked cities of Sodom and Gomorrah were burned to the ground. Some say that God was responsible . . ."
> Write an imaginary interview with a character in your Torah portion.
> Tell the story from the point of view of another character, or a minor character, in the story. For instance, tell the story of the Garden of Eden from the point of view of the serpent. Or the story of the Binding of Isaac from the point of view of the ram, which was substituted for Isaac as a sacrifice. Or perhaps the story of the sale of Joseph from the point of view of his coat, which was stripped off him and dipped in a goat's blood.
> Write a poem about your Torah portion.
> Write a song about your Torah portion.
> Write a play about your Torah portion, and have some friends act it out with you.
> Create a piece of artwork about your Torah portion.

The bottom line is: Make this a joyful experience. Yes—it could even be fun.

The Very Last Thing You Need to Know at This Point

The Torah scroll is written without vowels. Why? Don't *sofrim* (Torah scribes) know the vowels?

Of course they do.

So, why do they leave the vowels out?

One reason is that the Torah came into existence at a time when sages were still arguing about the proper vowels, and the proper pronunciation.

But here is another reason: The Torah text, as we have it today, and as it sits in the scroll, is actually *an unfinished work.* Think of it: the words are just sitting there. Because they have no vowels, it is as if they have no voice.

When we read the Torah publicly, we give voice to the ancient words. And when we find meaning in those ancient words, and we talk about those meanings, those words jump to life. They enter our lives. They make our world deeper and better.

Mazal tov to you, and your family. This is your journey toward Jewish maturity. Love it.

THE TORAH

❖ Va-'ethannan: Deuteronomy 3:23–7:11

This Torah portion begins with Moses recalling how he had pleaded with God to be allowed to cross over the Jordan River and to enter the Land of Israel. No go, says God. So, knowing that the end is coming sooner rather than later, Moses recounts the history of the Israelites so that they will be able to learn its lessons. He reminds them that God has been merciless to idolaters, and that the Israelites must worship God alone.

Jewish laws and teachings affect the reputation that the Jewish people will have, even though they have been conveyed by a God who has no form and only communicates through a voice. Finally, just so the Jewish people really understand, the parashah repeats the Ten Commandments here (an earlier version of them is in Exodus 20)—with a few minor, but significant changes.

This brings us to the *Shema,* the declaration of God's unity and uniqueness, along with specific ways to demonstrate love for God.

Summary

➤ Moses remembers how he had begged God to allow him to enter the Land of Israel. God had refused, but God showed him the land from afar. (3:23–29)
➤ Moses tells the people that God's laws are proof of God's greatness, and will be their way of creating a sacred standing among the nations. (4:6–8)
➤ Moses recalls the moment of Sinai. He reminds the people that they did not see God but only heard a voice. (4:11–14)
➤ Moses repeats the Ten Commandments—with a few changes. (5:6–18)
➤ Moses teaches about the uniqueness of God, and emphasizes that the Israelites must demonstrate their love for God through concrete actions. (6:4–9)

The Big Ideas

> **Arguing with God is an ancient Jewish tradition.** This is a common theme in the Torah and in later Jewish tradition. Abraham, Moses, Job, the various authors of the Psalms, various ancient sages, Hasidic teachers, and even Tevye in *Fiddler on the Roof* all argued with God.

> **Judaism is bigger than just the Jews.** Deuteronomy introduces a new idea: what Jews do has implications for the whole world, and Jewish teachings create the way that the world perceives Jews.

> **You cannot see God.** The People of Israel did not see God at Sinai; they only heard God. If they had seen God, they would have spent more time arguing over what God looked like, rather than arguing about the meaning of God's sacred words.

> **The Ten Commandments are so important that they appear twice.** But there are some minor changes in the Deuteronomy version. The version of them here in Deuteronomy says that Jews must observe Shabbat, as well as "remember" Shabbat. Moses says that slaves must also rest on Shabbat—conveying the growing sense that slaves are human beings, too. There is far more emphasis on how God took the Israelites out of Egypt—"with a mighty hand and an outstretched arm." Finally, God says that the Israelites are not only to refrain from coveting what others have, but are not to crave those things either. This makes the commandment even stronger.

> **Moses teaches that God is *echad*.** As most scholars admit, it is difficult to figure out what this word really means (in fact, thousands of pages have been written on the meaning of this small word). Whatever it means, the *Shema* has become "the watchword of the Jewish faith," and it has inspired Jews throughout history.

> **Jews must love God.** Love doesn't mean affection. It means a deep, powerful connection that binds Jews to God through the mitzvot.

Divrei Torah

THE MOST IMPORTANT SENTENCE IN JUDAISM

It is the most important sentence in the Torah. Okay, make that "in the entire Hebrew Bible." Come to think of it—make that "in all of Judaism." We are talking about the *Shema*—six Hebrew words *Shema Yisrael Adonai Eloheinu Adonai Echad* (6:4) that are sometimes referred to as "the watchword of the Jewish faith," or what the ancient sages called *kabbalat ol ha-Shamayim* (the acceptance of the yoke of Heaven).

It is the first sentence in Hebrew that a Jewish child learns. When Jews pray, they say it at morning worship (*Shacharit*) and at evening worship (*Ma'ariv*). It's also found in the Torah service. It's said at the end of Yom Kippur. Observant Jews say it when they go to sleep. And, just as it is the first Hebrew sentence that a child learns, so, too, it is the last Hebrew sentence that a Jew says.

The *Shema* is almost like a secret Jewish code. During World War II, there were many Jewish children who had been rescued by Christians and undercover Jews and who then spent the war hidden in monasteries. After the war, Rabbi Eliezer Silver went around Europe, looking for those children. He would visit those monasteries and simply say: *"Shema Yisrael . . ."* If a child completed the sentence, he would claim the child as a Jew.

But what does it mean when it says that "The Lord is one," *echad*? The possibilities are almost endless—just like God.

It could mean that there is only one god. Except in this stage of the Bible's development, the Torah itself seems to recognize that there are many nations that have many gods. Pure monotheism that insists that no other gods exist comes later in Judaism.

Second, it could mean that there is only one God, not numerically, but spiritually. Even though God seems "different" at different stages of Jewish history, God is always God. A midrash teaches: "I am the Lord your God—the same one who was in Egypt, the same one who was at the Red Sea, at Sinai, in the past and in the future, in this world and in the world to come."

Or, it could simply mean that Adonai is the only god whom Jews should worship. That increasingly accepted interpretation has led many, including the JPS TANAKH to translate the end of the *Shema* as "the Lord alone."

There is one more, controversial, theory: The whole word is a misprint! In ancient Hebrew, the letter *chet* could sometimes look like the letter *heh*. And the letter *dalet* could sometimes look like the letter *vet*. The Torah text was written by scribes and passed down from generation to generation. It would have been easy to make a mistake in copying the letters.

Professor David Sperling contends that the word *echad* was originally *ahav* (love): "Therefore, the real translation should be: Hear O Israel, Adonai is our God—love Adonai." This makes sense in that the very next words are, "And you shall love Adonai with all your heart."

The *Shema* is the most important line in Judaism, yet the debate on what it means goes on. That's Judaism for you!

LOVE GOD!

As you learned in Hebrew school, you can't have the *Shema* without the *Ve-ahavta*. That's what comes right after the *Shema* in both the worship service and in the Torah itself. The *Ve-ahavta* is also called *kabbalat ol ha-mitzvot* (the acceptance of the yoke of the mitzvot). The *Ve-ahavta* tells us that we should not only know that there is a God; we should love God, and that love should be manifest in specific actions.

What actions do we list aloud in the *Ve-ahavta*? One of them, most importantly, is "Teach them to your children." It is not enough to merely know these words; they must be transmitted to future generations. That is the meaning of Jewish continuity. In the words of the Israeli writer Fania Oz-Salzberger: "The great story and its imperatives passed from generation to generation on tablets, parchment and paper. As I check my references on an iPad, I realize that we have come full circle: from tablet to tablet, from scroll to scroll."

"Bind them as a sign upon your hand; let them be symbols before your eyes." Those are the tefillin (leather boxes containing words of Torah) that are worn during morning prayer on the forearm and on the forehead by traditional Jews.

"Inscribe them on the doorposts of your house and on your gates." That is the mezuzah that marks the doorposts of the Jewish home.

But you're probably thinking: okay, those are rituals and actions, but how can the Torah really tell us to love God? Isn't love an emotion? How can you command an emotion? Here, we need to learn from archeologists of the ancient Middle East. They tell us that when ancient kings made treaties (or covenants) with their underlings, the underlings were commanded to "love" the more powerful king. Love wasn't an emotional thing; the word "love" was used to symbolize loyalty.

But the early sages tell us that there is another dimension to love. It's not only to love God; it's also to inspire others to love God. "If someone studies Torah, and is honest in business, and speaks pleasantly to people, what do people say concerning him? 'Happy the father who taught him Torah, happy the teacher who taught him Torah!' But if someone studies Torah, but is dishonest in business, and discourteous in his relations with people, what do people say about him? 'Woe unto his father who taught him Torah; woe unto his teacher who taught him Torah!'"

To be a Jew, therefore, is to have awesome responsibility. It is to love God, and it is to be God's PR agent in the world.

Connections

> Have you ever thought that God was being unfair? What did you do about it? Did you talk to God, or even yell at God?

> Have you ever thought that what you do, as a Jew, affects people who are not Jewish? In what ways do you think Jewish laws and teachings can create a good impression on others?

> Do you agree that God is invisible? What would be the benefits of having a god that you could see? The disadvantages?

> What do you think of the changes that Moses made in the second version of the Ten Commandments? Do you agree with them? If you could make any changes, what would they be?

> What is your own interpretation of the *Shema*?

> What does it mean for you to love God?

THE HAFTARAH

❖ Va-ethannan: Isaiah 40:1–26

For most of the Jewish year, there is a thematic connection between the haftarah and the corresponding Torah portion. But starting with this Shabbat, and until we get to Rosh Hashanah, you can forget about such a connection. The *haftarah* for the entire book of Deuteronomy from here on will have almost nothing to do with their Torah portions.

Instead, they will have everything to do with this particular time of year. Start with the "holiday" that Jews observe this week—Tisha b'Av (the commemoration of the destruction of the Temple in Jerusalem). Then, count seven weeks, and we get to Rosh Hashanah. Seven is a special Jewish number, as in seven days of the week, or seven days for sitting shiva. That's exactly what we are doing here—sitting shiva for the independence of ancient Judea, while we imagine that God is visiting us, offering comfort.

That's why these weeks are called *sheva denechemta*—the seven weeks of consolation that follow Tisha b'Av. And it begins with this week, which has a special name: Shabbat Nachamu (Comfort). *Nachamu* is the first word of the haftarah.

During these seven weeks, all the *haftarah* come from the great prophet known as Second Isaiah, whose words appear in the book of Isaiah, chapters 40 through 66. His name was most likely not Isaiah, but his prophecies were added to the book of the earlier prophet Isaiah. This anonymous prophet lived in the period when the Babylonian Empire was coming to an end, and Persia was gaining in power. Second Isaiah sensed that even though the Jews were now in exile, they were about to come home. His words are full of hope for the Jewish people.

Cheer Up

If there were to be a name-recognition contest for prophets, Isaiah would win. He is the most famous of all the prophets, and his name is practically synonymous with the prophetic impulse in Judaism. That is certainly the case with the *haftarah* for *sheva denechemta*. They all come from the book of Isaiah—but remember, from the prophet known as Second Isaiah.

Rabbi Mark Dov Shapiro asks: "If the haftarah following Tisha B'Av are all devoted towards consolation and are taken from the book of Isaiah, on what basis were the specific verses for each of the seven sabbaths selected?" The question arises because the prophetic portions seem to have been chosen with no particular rhyme or reason.

Here's an intriguing answer to Rabbi Shapiro's question: Abudaraham, a commentator in the fourteenth century, believed that if you take the first verse of each of the seven *haftarah,* they form an imaginary conversation between God, the prophet, and the Jewish people.

Let's start with this week's haftarah portion. God tells the prophet: "Comfort, oh comfort my people" (40:1). God wants the people to know that their time of exile in Babylon is coming to an end, and that they will soon be able to return to the Land of Israel.

But, go to next week's haftarah. The people are not so sure that God really will fulfill that promise. "Zion says, 'The Lord has forsaken me, my Lord has forgotten me'" (49:14).

So, in the following week's haftarah, the prophet tells God that the people are "unhappy, storm-tossed one, uncomforted!" (54:11). God has to speak directly with the people. The next week's haftarah begins with God saying: "I, I am He who comforts you!" (51:12).

In the subsequent *haftarah,* God continues with personal reassurances. In the Bible, a woman who cannot have children is a symbol of hopelessness. And yet, in the fifth haftarah of consolation—"Shout, O barren one, you who bore no child!" (54: 1)—a hopeless people will find hope once again! The sixth week features God saying: "Arise, shine, for your light has dawned" (60:1). And by the seventh week, leading up to Rosh Hashanah, the people are emotionally ready to return to Zion: "I greatly rejoice in the Lord, my whole being exults in my God" (61:10).

Notice, by the way: the people cannot comfort themselves (much like infants who need others to comfort them). The prophet cannot do it alone. And God cannot do it alone. That is why these *haftarah* contain both God's words and the prophet's words. A midrash says: "The prophet came to God and said that the people refused to be comforted. God then said: 'Then you and I will go together to comfort them.'"

That's a provocative thought about cheering people up and giving them hope. Telling people to "keep the faith" perhaps is not enough, and being there for someone goes a long way, although maybe that too falls short. But a combination of both approaches just might do it.

❖ Notes

CPSIA information can be obtained
at www.ICGtesting.com
Printed in the USA
LVHW091832250319
611761LV00003B/407/P

9 780827 614550